OUTCROPPINGS
from Navajoland

OUTCROPPINGS
from Navajoland

poems by DONALD LEVERING

photographs by
Gregg D. Baker and Leonard Gorman

Navajo Community College Press

ACKNOWLEDGEMENTS

I thank the editors of the following publications, in which these poems first appeared:

Cottonwood Review, "Thunder Mesa"; *Mine Talk,* "The Giants"; *The New Mexico Independent,* "Mesa Walk," "Raven's Nest"; *Northwest Magazine,* "Silica"; *Portland Review,* "Notes from the Arroyo"; *Quindaro,* "Dust Devil"; *Sands,* "Sagebrush"; *Seven Stars Poetry,* "Remedy For Drought"; and *Star Web Paper,* "Sulphur Lake."

I thank Ann Baker and Paul Phelps for their assistance.

Designed by Linnea Gentry
Typesetting by Business Graphics, Inc.

International Standard Book Number 0-912586-52-4
Library of Congress Number 83-73475

for Janice

CONTENTS

I

SILICA

from a distance it seems
an indian has dashed
a bottle against
the mesa wall
smashing the monster
of delirium tremens
before it reappears—
but look closer Anglo
this transluscent rock
is laid in sheets
of luminescence
an icy fragment
lifted in the hand
is lens to the land
below, framed by Yei*
whose bodies comprised
rainbows
before the Flood
when the Navajo
ascended through a reed
to this Fifth Level
of horses, white men
and whiskey

**Yei (yā́-ē): primeval giants, often represented as rainbow
figures encompassing Navajo ritual sandpaintings*

CALCIUM PHOSPHATE   (Origin of Thunder)

in a previous world
lived men who resembled
giant ants
with egg-shaped heads
like the flute-player
petroglyphs

              they built mounds
& lived in darkness
but when lightning flasht
the insides of their hives
brightened so
that they were blinded
& dasht between bolts
knocking heads

              you still can see
where the downpour
of the Flood
washt their smasht skulls
to the surface

F O S S I L S

branded in rock, this star
must have fallen from the sky
consider the mesa's elevation
its distance from the sea

locked in stone, it cooled to form
the handprint of an ape
who lived on piñon nuts
and slept under a million candles

one must have dripped intelligence
among these barren stones
here is a shape like a brain,
kidney, embroyo

but how can one mistake
the spiraling form
of sea snail, coiling
down millenniums

and who could doubt
the earth's upheaval
or the sea's receding
since this turtle

toppled and left
a basin that fills
with stars
after rain

T U M B L E W E E D   (*Salsola kali*)

autumn they are done w/ the
staid life of shrubs, their
anchors left to plumb the
desert depths while they roll
away rootless on billows,
tumbling toward boulders,
dropping into arroyos,
bouncing across highways,
stacking against fences
always sowing seeds

SAGEBRUSH   *(Artemisia tridentata)*

pungent acres
where no two plants touch
if the wind will grant
a few fists of rain
they'll hold their ground
shadows quivering
around them
their yellow blooms of August
offspring of the sun

REMEDY FOR DROUGHT

Osha
Root of the Chuskas
A gift strung
On bead thread
Hung above the threshold
House talisman

Ambrosia
Steeping in my tea

Your compass flower
Nodded south, drew
Dragonflies, bees
Stitching thistle
Blooms, a Zuni woman
Toting a bag of roots

Your burled toes stretched
Deep under desert
Into mineral waters
She yanked &
Held your string of rhizomes
In her callused hands

Emetic brew

Flushes the pheasant
From the tongue's
Underbrush
(thus the woman was named
She Who Finds Fowl)

The ventriloquial
Owl calling
Is Osha presence
Its tremolo
Falls as cactus
Blossoms close

Emollient
Softens hooves

II

LAVA BEDS *(The Malpais)*

Pines and cholla
grow through this dark
stone ocean. Navajos say
it is a great pool
of dried blood
from a dangerous giant
beheaded by Twin Brothers.
The black rock draws
sun into its blood,
lava heaving for miles,
cholla and pines
feeding on that old feud.
& off in the rippling distance
how cool those shoulders
that have forgotten
in the snow.

THE BISTI *

the sagebrush ends here
where the inland sea
last retreated
carving strange forms

in its wake
barren landscape
of mushroom rocks
and petrified trunks

of cypress
creatureless
but for racoon tracks
and the tiny bones and beaks

compressed into owl pellets
the conchiform tunnels
and living stones
jam the mental compass

though coal spills
from former lives
only wind can tell
where the Old Ones are buried

or precisely where
among these whistling spans
the Navajo emerged
from the Flood

*bĭś-tī: the Navajo Badlands

SULPHUR LAKE

Below the mesas of Zuni
smelled before seen
the yellow lake
ringed from evaporation
sulphur upwelling.

———————————————

The old man told
that a long time ago
one of the Giants,
Grasshopper Man,
devoured all the unripe
beans in Zuni gardens.
He got sick & duckt
into a sweatlodge.
Many days he spent
crouching by the steaming
rocks, until the other Giants
got sick of his belching
& farting & kickt him
out. Grasshopper Man
emerged dizzy & trippt
on a mesa; almost falling,
he reached down for balance
& touched earth, right here,
where this sweaty
stinking thumbprint is.
Now all grasshoppers are
skinny, just elbows & knees,
from his having the shits
so bad, and we are left
with this smelly pond.

ZUNI SALT LAKE DEPOSIT

The procession would leave at night
with their digging spoons
following grains of salt
in the sky, arriving at Tall House
with dawn, there being
offered saltless soup
boiled by hot rocks.
Motes of dust would lead
that afternoon into the trail
of stars again, their eyes
tearing from wind.
The moon would be shrinking
these nights, so when
they finally filed down
from the mesas, its wedge
would be right for digging.
The parched tongue of the
lost lake dazzled like snow-light.
They filled their yucca-baskets
with thanks and turned back
toward Pueblo Bonito.

KIN YA'A RUINS

Fragments from an Anasazi Refuse Dump

water currents
or flames
painted on an oval
river-bed stone
hauled here to boil
pottage

———————

black thunderbolt
jagged shard

———————

ash
from old watchfires
from dancers' thighbones

———————

vanisht stream of feet
flows in pavingstone

———————

by a smasht skull
the chippt lip
of a jug
the broken *O*
of a vowel shift
the culture collapsing

———————

piece of a bowl
tumbled kiva

———————

vase fragment
hauled to the empress
of ants

———————

hunger spoon
tongued thin
in drought moons

———————

sweat-stained bead
seed of a stanza
to a forgotten song
tarnisht star of a
lost constellation

———————

burnt beans
on a pot
dasht to bits

———————

kachina doll
shrunken to toothless
grandpa of cottonwood root

———————

obsidian earring

———————

clay with painted
black coils
of snakes or goddess'
locks

———————

antler handle

———————

toad
still as stone
spotted
soft
watches
with its sacred eye

———————

gibbous moon of a vessel
held juniper berry juice
for cramps
crackt eggshell pattern

———————

thousand year old
corn kernal
kept in a cricket cage
unearthed
sprouts
roots through chamber pot
grows to the sun
pollen raining down

THUNDER MESA

in the sheer rock wall
a single fissure
jagged as lightning
admits mortals to the mesa rim

> from here the canyons
> fall away in great
> crankling gashes

the lichens feed
on the colors of sleet
crystals ticking
boulders split by
juniper and piñon

> far beneath the memory
> of nautilus tattooed
> in stone
> cactus roots strike water

here a bleached limb
is a goat-horn
this the plain
where thunder dances

> these the charred and
> palsied limbs
> root-balls flaring
> drummed out of the rock

THE NIGHT WAY*

lightning sleeps with spooled snakes
as piñon fires boil
before brush shelters
a palsied man (who may
have crossed Coyote)
has sought a healer's aid
in a circle dance the Yei

_____

inside the hogan
sitting in the center
of the First World
diagrammed in sand
he is sung over
bathed in yucca suds
then the floor is swept
another stream
of tinted sand
falls from
forefinger and thumb
of the medicine man
painting another world
on the dirt floor
the patient is centered
sung
and cleansed again

_____

the seventh night of ceremony
in a circle dance the Yei
muffled whoops come through their masks—

*a winter ceremony, in this case, the Yei-bi-chei

a spine of juniper snaps
Coyote relinquishes the victim's limbs
the dance continues

_____

until the bluebird song of dawn
is sung
and the patient walks surely
with a prayer stick
into the rising sun

III

RAVEN'S NEST

a bundle of piñon sticks
          stuffed with scraps
          of tin, tatters of
          cloth, aluminum tops,
          silver concha belt
bunched into a nook
at the mesa's rim

downwind in the bloody dusk
the reek of carrion

this nest a desert broom
sweeping the sage clean
of refuse, what coyote
left of the lamb
the litter of humans

like huge Jurassic wasps
the ravens come and go
in blue-black streaks
from their rookery
child-stealing witches
in the eyes of Navajos

a raven swings out from the cliff
not croaking, just the slow
pulse of wingbeats

                              thew

          thew

thew

CAR HULK

wedged in arroyo bedrock
weirdest fossil
peyote ever saw
Mesozoic dung-beetle

imagine it nudging
a flaming ball
of diplodocus dung

this scene gone
the way of the stream
as peyote-vision fades—
old Hudson returns to the gulley

stove-in roof
rabbitbrush engine
its trunk bristling
with scent of sage
seatsprings like rattlers' rings

but its husk still burns
the colors of mesas
at dusk

BEER CAN CAIRN

```
              *
          *   *
        *       *
       shining
      * nose of a *
    slurred constellation *
    false fire in the desert *
  aluminum under a drunken moon *
    * years from now will still point
    to a blurry star * * someone will
  wonder what ritual accompanied the
    stacking of another can * * * in a
  distant century the pile may have risen
 higher than Hosta Butte when another tongue
 asks * * whose altar * * whoever they were * they
 * stumbled away in stellar winds like luck candles *
```

ANTHILL

crazed by the Flood
or thunder
busy red bugs
obsessed with building
condominiums
& biting the flesh
of barefoot boys

———————

somewhere deep under
a knee-high mound
of coarse tailings
reigns the Queen
with her hoard
of nuggets
mother & lover
of thousands

———————

stare at their boil
in the ground
all goes red like
staring at the sun
under clouds

———————

a cherry-bomb explodes
at the lip & ants pour
like lava from the cone
thunder-struck
they resume construction
& biting little boys

URANIUM TAILINGS

the pile
reflects
the heat
of human hands
what other creature
would spread the entrails
of Mother Earth over the land

and in the disemboweling
the whirling drilling rig
has left this mound of scat
to wash into rivers like mud
to lift into lungs like dust
to tear into flesh like Toothed Rocks*

*a monster of landscape that had to be overcome by the Hero Twins

DUST DEVIL

not like in Kansas
where tornadoes can
twist your house to splinters
more like the pattern
in a Navajo rug
that captures your eye
& would trap your soul
if the weaver hadn't first
found her own way out
but while your eyes were busy
with the dancing sandspout
a corporate geologist
was drilling for uranium
now the devil turns &
throws sand in your eyes
while the weaver signs
the land away for the promise
of a paved road to her hogan
next he sucks
the wells dry
& leaves a pile of poison

KACHINA DOLL SALESMAN

Door to door selling gods
hewn from cottonwood root
he limps. The children of
incest,* riding piggy-back,
with heads like deformed jars,
go fast. The bird-beaked
house-warming god** is also
popular with his Anglo buyers.
Before TV, these dolls
told stories of larger gods
who shaped and painted our world.
Now the pueblo children
watch cartoons, believing
only in the gifts the big
kachinas bring on dance days.
The bandy-legged craftsman
offers these vestiges
of belief too cheaply,
but the hours spent fixed
on root, knife, and paintbrush
he dwelled in myth. To us
he hands a sun-god,
abstract disk of a face
wreathed in quail-feathers,
with a turquoise-studded belt,
who wields a tiny gourd rattle
that shook thunder in ages past.

*mudheads   **Shalako

C O A L

    coal seam
              leviathan of carbon
                        snakes the canyon
             how green this place
must have been
             ferns tall as firs
                    steaming brontosaurus
                        turds
                  big as cows
      green dolphins bouncing songs
                  off these cliffs
    nosing back into this inland sea

—————————————————

    levithan's black blood
    spills from mesa walls
    as buckets big as hogans
    dredge coal from these old shallows

    Ahab smokes in his diesel cab

—————————————————

    from Mount Powell

    the mine appears to be
                   a sea-snail
            or leviathan's tail
         shunted by train
       to feed the old
     fire-story
   a tale beginning
with a miner's bloody nose

THE GIANTS

mesas strewn across the land
like giants' limbs
cut by wind & water
to the marrow: coal-veins
exposed

Navajos have endured
the cutting of a road
across the sacred trail
of the Giant's blood
from Mount Taylor
to their heartland

will they persevere
after their graves
are stripped for coal
& the turquoise & silver skies
have gone to smoke
after the gas is tapped
the oil bled
after uranium dust
has settled
glowing in their bones
after the copper mountains
south & west
have been leveled
for the nervous giant
of electricity

IV

THREE WAYS
TO HIKE HIGH MESA COUNTRY

climb until your lungs heave
like raven wingbeats
sidle through a crack
at the mesa's rim, plant
your hands on a ledge and
pull your weight to it, then
pull yourself to the top—
still heaving, you have gained

the wind's way over mesas
your blusht face the color
of lichens growing here
on wind-lickt boulders

when your breath returns
begin to skirt the ridge
with wind at your heels, your
eyes tracing the folds
of arroyos, the San Juans looming,
the clean smell of junipers

---

maybe draw a line
in the mind's eye
from here to destination
heedless of wind, climb, snakes,
cockle-burrs, tarantulas
but straight
across talus, one leg
drained of blood, the other ankle
sprained
huffing up and down ridges
under tomes of rock
that could crush you
unmindful of scorpions
behind each stone

---

or you could read the water's
petroglyphs
as you follow the curves
of arroyo, the slow
path into canyons
where the wind
whistles the turns
in your circuitous
smooth road
of rainwater,
clambering over boulders
made easy
with the force of
tomorrow's gulleywasher
behind you

THE CRUMBLING MESA

every morning I gaze
at the crumbling mesa-face
trying to know
which rock
came down with the night
each day the same high
cheekbones of stone
radiate dawn
yet something
has fallen
in my sleep

a crevasse has widened
imperceptibly
a boulder has begun
to look down
a ledge has shifted

soundlessly a stone
has slipped from above
as I slept
and in the dust
risen to the glass
my wrinkled brow reflects

TRAIL TO THE LAND-BRIDGE

for my father and Marti

April — the trail of
thorns through
blooming prickly pears
past the circle of
bleached limbs
        braced
   with bedsprings
 forming a goat pen

billy-goat horns
hang on the gate

farther up
     & off the path
  at the mesa's rim
 a stone hogan
 the sun climbs
 like a wild rose

————

later I learned
this abandoned circle
of stones
at the precipice
was a *chindi** dreaded
house of the dead
I was warned
under the ashes of
vagabond camps within
rest the bones
of a Navajo shepherd

————

* *chĭń-dē*

50

September — the trail
of fuming sagebrush
past the goat pen
        the living shepherd's tent
my daughter testing
                        the heft
of certain stones
                the scent
of crushed sage

                lightning
splits the fissures
of our skulls
fear spills out
filling the sudden clouds
spitting in the dust
                    thunder rumbles
all around
        a bolt strikes the land-bridge

stacking branches across
the roofless chindi
we find shelter
squatting in the ashes
of its cold hearth
under skeletons
exposed in the sky

CHAMELEON *(Iguana anolis)*

Not my will that killed you
but driven wheels
the illusion-puddled
pavement, the highway
a lizard tail
between mesas,
the car knowing
no limit to sage
and speed. A ghost
from a burned
roadside hogan
stuttered your limbs—
a soulless lizard
would have skittered
straight across
the hot concrete.
The whining tires
that mesmerized
like a rattler's eyes
cannot be blamed
on me; I do not
animate machines.
Your perfect dance
of vascillation,
the rainbows
of your flesh
in the instant
before death
were your decision.
The ugly thud
of bad luck
is mine.

CANYON DE CHELLY* —
WHITE HOUSE TRAIL

for Chip Goodrich

snow at the rim
but our eyes' descent
through millennia
of stone
to the river's thread
below
catches the breath

———————

being beneath the body
the feet can only follow
the steep trail
down
yet gravity
cannot keep Chip's eyes
from rising
to eddies of sandstone
cliffs
as we achieve
perfect vertigo
at each switch-
back

near the bottom
the trail turns
fearful
melted snow
has muddied the path
through a tunnel
that banishes sunlight

*da shāy

and turns thoughts back
to de Chelly
in the garb of an
unclaimed ancestor
sergeant in Carson's army
pursuing Navajos
                        between these steep faces
torching hogans and orchards
but finding no indians
until dusk
when a thousand campfires
mock us from the rim

————————

we walk away
from a billion years
of stone overhead
                        afternoon light
spills onto the canyon floor
cookstove smoke rises
through a survivor's hogan
a million water-shoots
                        the winter growth
                            of willows

        shimmer

the glint of water
seen from the rim
stretches before us
a frozen stream
                imagine a freshet
                with the verve
                to cut such a canyon
its surface gleams
tentative crystals

winter lightning
in the ice
under feet

                    sliding above the current
by the grace of the gods
                    my eyes
people the pockets
of sandstone cliffs
with rooks
                    impossible
fossils
            dinosaur eggs

_____

how surprising
and how natural
the pueblo called
White House
        appears

under a massive overhang
of red rock
like the nest
of mud daubers
a thousand years ago
Anasazi women
ground corn here
children played cat's cradle
with willow withes
men smoked and watched
the falling of the daily
shadow from the south wall
across the plaza

what a place
for a human hive
                         the snowy rim
                         a season behind
this sun-facing adobe
             my friend
      meditates
I peel off layers of clothes
orange rind
              and brush away
      mid-winter flies

———————

sheep bells
float through my drowse
the Navajo herder's
clicking tongue
signals his sheep
from this house of ghosts

Chip
seems to
quit breathing
all solar plexus
he leans toward
the convex

overhang
       under a hawk
            hitching thermals

finally discerning
footholds
in the rock
to the rim
         where the ghost
        of a Navajo sorcerer
       conjured apparitions
      before the Spanish Captain
    camped below
who turned his troops back

_____

something calls
           shepherd
     or
swallow

_____

leaving the ruins
by the same trail
of armies
in dazed retreat upstream
past the looming monolith
                s
                p
                i
                d
                e
                r
                r
                o
                c
                k
where the weavers' mentor
        spider-woman
           dwells

resting at the rim
we enter the long thoughts
of sheer rock faces
where swallow-nesting peoples
have hewn footholds
between worlds

                      the one a repeating
                      chronicle
                      of futile conquest

           of the other
hidden in de Chelly's
stone vaults
glimpsed in petroglyphs

          where deer

                             imps
flute-players

            dance

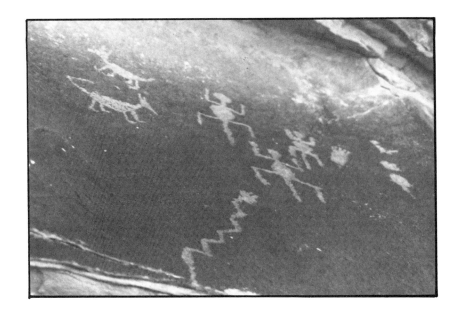

MESA WALK

steep climb up the mesa-face
past the painted molar-stone
    the water-carved heart
I slip through a crevasse
like a lizard
           to the mesa's rim
           panting on top of a world
           worn to stone & sand
           crackt by juniper roots
           where wind polishes
           the howling dolmens
           & ravens hurl to earth
           like black holes

a covey of quail
scurries from snappt
piñon twigs underfoot
past cairns stackt here
by thundershowers
         a cottontail
flees my bootsteps
         heading toward
the land-bridge
    between mesas

the quiet eye
of a prickly pear
aims for my heel
a prairie rattler
slides toward my body's heat

from up here
         on the land-bridge
a man could fall forever
         into canyons
coyote could nudge him over

EVENING AT CROWNPOINT, NEW MEXICO

No longer molten-red with sunset
the mesa still radiates
the day's heat
as the desert
cools. In my teacup
float the evening stars
of ephedra flowers,
the scent of sagebrush
still on my fingertips.
A campfire flares
at the mesa's rim,
and I remember following
an overgrown path
up there, crushing
sage tips and sniffing,
letting myself be led
to an excavation
shaped like a sweat-lodge.
I pictured steaming
rocks and red-faced men
forcing bad humours
from their pores. Or,
timbered-over, a root-cellar
for squash and corn.
But a gust from the west
dispersed these visions,
and only a mound of
sandy soil and a hole
in the earth remained.
I picked ephedra and gazed
at toppled ponderosas
bleached like driftwood.

Afloat on the high mesa,
at one with sage and ephedra,
I told myself
this is a place
to be quiet, the
prickly pears still
flaring scarlet
in July

follow the goat-prints
in dry sand
up the arroyo
into the fluted canyon

why should your shadow
leave you standing
at this confluence
unable to choose
which water-route
your body should follow

where have the hooves flown
that have disappeared
up impossible cliffs

who has swallowed the sun

will the magpie
stitching the canyon
sell your skin to coyote

another fork
go
contrary
take the sand-river
left
chew
what the goats have left
of datura
& slink like a shadow
through lichen-painted boulders
against a torrent of wind

the canyon breaks into
broad stream bed
whose rocks have been panning
the sun's gold
centuries
breathe easier
the wind has quit mourning
hear your own song
curving over stone

DONALD LEVERING recently lived in Navajoland for two years, teaching extension courses for Navajo Community College. He received a Master of Fine Arts in Creative Writing from Bowling Green State University where he was also a Devine Memorial Fellow and poetry editor of *The Penny Dreadful*. His first chapbook, *The Jack of Spring*, was published by Swamp Press in 1980. Another chapbook, *Carpool*, is forthcoming from Tellus. Mr. Levering currently lives in Santa Fe, New Mexico.

GREGG D. BAKER, formerly of Crownpoint, New Mexico, is a painter and photographer now residing in Denver, Colorado.

LEONARD GORMAN is a photographer from Chinle, Arizona. He is a junior at the University of Kansas in Lawrence.